SPLINTER

BY HILARY BELL

CURRENCY PRESS
The performing arts publisher

CURRENT THEATRE SERIES

First published in 2019
by Currency Press Pty Ltd,
PO Box 2287, Strawberry Hills, NSW, 2012, Australia
enquiries@currency.com.au
www.currency.com.au

in association with Griffin Theatre Company

Copyright: *Splinter* © Hilary Bell, 2012, 2019.

COPYING FOR EDUCATIONAL PURPOSES
The Australian *Copyright Act 1968* (Act) allows a maximum of one chapter or 10% of this book, whichever is the greater, to be copied by any educational institution for its educational purposes provided that that educational institution (or the body that administers it) has given a remuneration notice to Copyright Agency (CA) under the Act.
For details of the CA licence for educational institutions contact CA, 11/66 Goulburn Street, Sydney, NSW, 2000; tel: within Australia 1800 066 844 toll free; outside Australia 61 2 9394 7600; fax: 61 2 9394 7601; email: info@copyright.com.au

COPYING FOR OTHER PURPOSES
Except as permitted under the Act, for example a fair dealing for the purposes of study, research, criticism or review, no part of this book may be reproduced, stored in a retrieval system, or transmitted in any form or by any means without prior written permission. All enquiries should be made to the publisher at the address above.

Any performance or public reading of *Splinter* is forbidden unless a licence has been received from the author or the author's agent. The purchase of this book in no way gives the purchaser the right to perform the play in public, whether by means of a staged production or a reading. All applications for public performance should be addressed to RGM, 8-12 Ann Street, Surry Hills NSW 2010, Australia; ph: +61 2 9281 3911.

Typeset by Dean Nottle for Currency Press.
Cover design by Alphabet.
Cover shows Simon Gleeson and Lucy Bell. Cover photo by Brett Boardman.

Currency Press acknowledges the Traditional Owners of the Country on which we live and work. We pay our respects to all Aboriginal and Torres Strait Islander Elders, past and present.

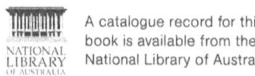
A catalogue record for this book is available from the National Library of Australia

Contents

SPLINTER 1

Theatre Program at the end of the playtext

Splinter was first produced as *The Splinter* by Sydney Theatre Company at Wharf 1 Theatre, Sydney, on 10 August 2012 with the following cast:

MAN	Erik Thomson
WOMAN	Helen Thomson
SHADOW TWINS / LAURA	Julia Ohannessian, Kate Worsley

Director, Sarah Goodes
Puppetry and Movement Director, Alice Osborne
Designer, Renee Mulder
Lighting Designer, Damien Cooper
Composer, Emily Maguire
Sound Designer, Steve Francis

CHARACTERS

MAN
WOMAN
SHADOW TWINS
LAURA

AUTHOR'S NOTE

Splinter was conceived with the idea that Laura is played by a Bunraku-style puppet. In the first production, she was manipulated by two actor/puppeteers. These women not only controlled Laura, but their presence provided a mysterious and unsettling note. They were invisible to the couple until the Man's doubt started to grow: he then became aware of them. At the point when he asks Laura 'Where is my daughter?', the puppet vanished and one of them took its place. The other then replaced her during the hair-brushing scene.

The Woman remained oblivious to the usurpations; the Man was deeply disturbed by them.

These two puppeteers became the Shadow Twins of Scene 24.

In the last scene, it was the puppet Laura that the Woman brought to him. The manipulators worked Laura until the final moment, where the Man is alone with her.

Puppetry was explored in a variety of ways throughout the production (there were two other 'Laura' puppets of a radically different scale; the 'absence' was represented by an empty dress, et cetera).

This note is offered in the spirit of suggestion, and is by no means meant to be prescriptive.

LAYOUT

Indented text indicates soliloquy, as opposed to dialogue. These lines are thoughts spoken for the benefit of the audience, unheard by other characters.

HB

1.

A MAN *in love with an absence.*

2.

MAN: Where is she?
WOMAN: In the bath, she's fine, I just checked.
...
...
MAN: My God.
WOMAN: Oh.
MAN: I know.
WOMAN: It's all over.
MAN: Yes.
...
MAN: Are you crying or laughing?
WOMAN: Laughing. Crying from laughing.
MAN: I'm amazed we have any tears left.
WOMAN: Everything's amazing, why are we surprised?
MAN: I am awake, tell me, aren't I, I couldn't bear it—
WOMAN: Yes, it's real.
MAN: Not a dream, because I did dream this, over and over.
WOMAN: It's real.
MAN: Isn't it dangerous leaving a four-year-old in the bath?
WOMAN: Five now. She's big enough, I only put a bit of water.
MAN: I can't sit down, I can't keep still, I'm going to check on her.
WOMAN: She doesn't want us to.
MAN: How do you know, did she—?
WOMAN: The door.
MAN: She shut the door on you?
WOMAN: Quietly.
MAN: I'm glad we got the radio fixed because I was crying my eyes out, all the way down, did you notice? I could hardly see the road.
WOMAN: That's why you kept turning up the volume.
MAN: You were in the back, you couldn't see me, I was howling. What was she doing?

WOMAN: Looking out the window, then she slept. I just held her.
MAN: I saw you crying too, in the mirror.
WOMAN: I thought I'd never be happy again. I thought I'd never smile. I never thought I'd be like this, trying to stop from bursting.
MAN: She's so, she's all …
WOMAN: I know!
MAN: It was a shock.
WOMAN: My first thought was, 'That's not Laura, not *my* Laura.'
MAN: She's so long.
WOMAN: Her arms and legs.
MAN: I was shocked.
WOMAN: That awful coat she was wearing.
MAN: And her face, what about her face—?
WOMAN: Exposure.
MAN: It's all puffy.
WOMAN: It'll go down.
MAN: And mature, don't you think?
WOMAN: Time.
MAN: And experience.
…
Maybe.
I walked in and sitting beside the policeman was this thin, long girl, arms folded, looking at the floor. I knew it was her, but for a moment—
WOMAN: It's like my arms ache when she's not in them, they're throbbing.
MAN: I held her and sobbed, and said, 'Is it really you, Laura?'
WOMAN: But we can't carry on too much or we'll scare her. She didn't say anything then, did she?
MAN: Just looked at me.
WOMAN: We have to be normal.
MAN: Yes.
WOMAN: Normal and calm. And maybe eventually—
MAN: She'll speak.
WOMAN: We won't push.
MAN: No.
WOMAN: We can bear anything now, a bit of waiting—
MAN: Who cares?
WOMAN: We've survived this.
MAN: We survived because of you.

WOMAN: Both of us.
MAN: No, you. You held us together.
WOMAN: But you were the one who wouldn't give up, you're why she's here.
MAN: I could only do that because of your strength. That first week—
WOMAN: Don't, let's forget all that.
MAN: No, but—
WOMAN: What did you think, that I'd leave you?
MAN: Her, and then me, in one week. How did you function?
WOMAN: You in hospital gave me something to do. I could do something about that.
MAN: Out of the clinic and straight to the liquor cabinet. I wouldn't have blamed you if you'd gone.
WOMAN: Stop.
MAN: We came close.
WOMAN: But we didn't.
MAN: Imagine if she'd come back to find she didn't have a home.
WOMAN: She's here, and we're all together.
MAN: I always believed she was alive, but whether we'd see her again—that thought sucked all the breath out of me, that she might be gone forever.
WOMAN: Once I lay down on the train track. I never told you. I drove out to the suburbs at dusk, when the light makes it hard to see. And I lay down.
MAN: What stopped you?
WOMAN: What if she'd knocked on the door and I wasn't there?
MAN: I'm glad you didn't tell me.
WOMAN: I wanted to.
MAN: But you didn't.
WOMAN: It would've been selfish.
MAN: No.
WOMAN: Yet another thing to bear.
MAN: Something must have been watching over us to make sure we stayed the course.
WOMAN: I think so, a divine presence.
MAN: Are you getting all Goddy on me?
WOMAN: An angel.
MAN: All New-Agey on me?

WOMAN: Well, what do you think it was?
MAN: Come here.
WOMAN: Shh.
MAN: I love you. I'm happy. We haven't kissed for nine months. Kiss me.
WOMAN: Stop tickling me.
MAN: I love you, I love you, I love you.

3.

MAN: I made your favourite, tomato soup. First time in—
And the bread too, still hot. Lots of butter.
Don't want to try it?
WOMAN: Maybe she's not hungry.
MAN: That's alright.
WOMAN: Did we bring tomatoes? There couldn't have been any growing, they're out of season.
MAN: I bought lots, because it's Laura's favourite soup.
How's yours?
WOMAN: Good, delicious.
MAN: —
WOMAN: —
MAN: It's nice and cosy indoors, isn't it?
WOMAN: Doesn't look like there's anyone else around, I can't see any lights.
MAN: Too cold for the beach. We've got it all to ourselves.
WOMAN: —
WOMAN: We'll—   MAN: I could make—
MAN: Sorry, you go.
WOMAN: You.
MAN: I could make something else. Sausages.
WOMAN: The soup's fine. We'll have to get Laura some new pyjamas, you've grown out of those old ones.
MAN: When we get back.
WOMAN: That's what I meant.
MAN: —
WOMAN: Dad wants us to come up.
MAN: You're getting reception?
WOMAN: Now and then. He wants to see her.
MAN: Of course. Not yet though.

WOMAN: That's what I said. I said when we get back.
MAN: That soon?
WOMAN: Put yourself, you know, he really wants to see her.
MAN: Yes, but this is our time.
WOMAN: He needs that too.
MAN: Remember Poppy? He never stopped talking about you.
WOMAN: If we say two weeks, we shouldn't change it.
MAN: Okay.
WOMAN: —
MAN: Supposed to rain for the next few days.
WOMAN: —
MAN: It doesn't matter, we don't need to go out. Isn't it nice to be here again? We haven't been to the house—
WOMAN: No, not for ages.
MAN: Pretty dusty. Garden's completely overgrown. The roses have borers and black spot. Roses, in winter, is that strange?
Slugs have eaten all the herbs.
WOMAN: Eggshells.
MAN: What?
WOMAN: Crush them and put them around the plants, the slugs can't get to them.
MAN: I brushed my hand against a twig tonight, very lightly, and down fell hundreds of brilliant insects. I wish you could've seen. Won't you just have one bite?
WOMAN: She will when she wants to.
MAN: Maybe it's not your favourite anymore. That's alright. You can eat bread with lots of butter, even though that's not a 'proper dinner', whatever that is, but we're on holiday and we can do whatever we like. You don't have to do a single thing you don't want to. We could even have dessert first, ice-cream and then soup, let's do that tomorrow. We're just so happy, there aren't words, so thankful to have you home, our dearest darling sweet girl. Come to me.
WOMAN: I didn't pack ice-cream, it would've melted.
MAN: If ice-cream's what you want, we'll find it.
WOMAN: Where?
MAN: We've got that freezer bag.
WOMAN: It'd still melt, it's too far.

MAN: Ice-cream once we're home, then. Enjoy what there is here. We'll go for a walk tomorrow, play in the garden.
WOMAN: Laura, if you go in the garden, you remember to stay inside the fence?
MAN: She won't be out of our sight.
WOMAN: Don't go out the gate. No climbing down the cliffs, no playing on the beach. And you mustn't wade out to your rock no matter how safe it looks, because the tide might come in.
MAN: She won't be out of our sight.
WOMAN: She's eating.
MAN: Yes.
WOMAN: She's eating your soup. That's a good sign.
MAN: It is, isn't it?

4.

WOMAN: He won't come to bed, but sits up watching over her. And I sleep better than I've ever slept.
MAN: I sit by her bed and watch her sleep. The puffiness is going. I can see Laura more clearly now, though her face has changed. It's like when she was a tiny baby and I would keep a vigil. I feared that if I took my eyes away, even for a moment, that soft rise and fall would stop. There's nothing I'd rather do than sit beside her and gaze. Those hellish days I could keep myself busy, I was on a quest, but the nights … I would sit by her bed and stare at an absence.
I learnt to love that absence like it was Laura herself.
WOMAN: He watches through the night, and in the morning instead of tired, he's serene, almost euphoric.
MAN: I was overcome at dinner, perhaps it was too much, I said, 'Come to me'. She stayed quite still, and stiff and cold. My poor lamb.
I superimpose the old Laura onto the face of the new.
I don't want to forget that face.

5.

The MAN *tries to abandon the absence.*

6.

A presence.

MAN: What?! What's wrong?!
WOMAN: Ahh—
MAN: Darling?
WOMAN: No, oh.
MAN: A nightmare?
WOMAN: I was awake. Oh God. I thought I saw someone looking in.
MAN: Where, in the window?
   Where are you going?
WOMAN: Laura.
   …
MAN: She's there?
WOMAN: Asleep. Oh, my heart, feel it.
MAN: What did you see?
WOMAN: Something moving. You can't sleep either, can you?
MAN: Not yet.
WOMAN: Did you see?
MAN: Maybe it was the shadows of trees.
WOMAN: Maybe.
MAN: It's windy tonight and there's a moon.
WOMAN: Yes.
   She has to sleep in here.
MAN: She doesn't want to.
WOMAN: I can't close my eyes, every sound …
MAN: I tried to get her to sleep in our bed, remember?, then I brought her mattress in; she wanted her own room. I think that's good, we mustn't smother her.
   Come on.
WOMAN: My heart's still racing.
MAN: Shh.
WOMAN: It's not really over, is it?
MAN: Let's take one moment at a time.
WOMAN: Are the windows all shut?
MAN: It wasn't here, darling, that was at home.

WOMAN: We'll move, now she's back again we can move. I can't live in that house anymore.
MAN: Alright.
WOMAN: Are they shut?
MAN: It's cold, we would've shut them.
WOMAN: I have to check.
MAN: I'll do it.
WOMAN: *Me. I have to check.*
MAN: Don't open the front door.

…

> Who are they? A man? A couple? A group? They're in her head, so they're in this house. They're at the table with us, in her bed. They come for walks with the three of us. They have a relationship with her that we know nothing about, they share things with her we'll never be privy to. They're still more real to her than we are, you can see that. We're a vague memory, a distant dream. She's obliged to be as overjoyed as we are, but it's an effort.

…

All shut and locked?
WOMAN: Yes. Gosh, it's freezing.
MAN: Your feet are wet: you didn't go outside?
WOMAN: I wanted to make sure.
MAN: Oh, love, that was bloody stupid!
WOMAN: No tyre marks.
MAN: If you don't care about yourself, what about me and Laura?
WOMAN: Don't get cross.
MAN: Maybe we should go home.
WOMAN: Do you want to go home?
MAN: No, do you?
WOMAN: No, but there are more people around.
MAN: What if there was no-one out there and we left before we wanted to?
WOMAN: I can't live like this.
MAN: It's not good for her, either. We think we're keeping her safe—she'll probably end up running away.
WOMAN: But the alternative's out of the question. What about when she goes to school, how will we get through the day? I'll never let her

walk to the corner shop no matter how old she is. We don't even know what we're fighting. Be careful of what?
MAN: Shh. Calm down. It's alright.
What are you doing?
WOMAN: Going into her bed.
MAN: No, come on—
WOMAN: I'll be able to sleep.
MAN: Love—
WOMAN: I'm fine.
MAN: Alright, goodnight.
...

> Come on then, I'm here, I'm at the window, waiting for you. Show me who you are. I can do it, one eye on you and one on my child. Let me see you once and I can burn through your skull just by thinking, I'll never stop thinking. Burn holes into your brain, cook your vile brain, then it'll be you begging, 'Let me go'.

7.

MAN: A tea party! Can I play?
Excuse me, Miss Laura, but can I play too?
... Here, give me the teapot. Let me pour.
Shouldn't we pour into a cup? You've got lovely little cups here ...
No? Into an eggshell, well, alright.
What's this, sand? No, yum, what nice tea.
I'm not supposed to drink it? Well, what do you want me to do?
—
Don't you want me to play?
—
—
Laura. Do you remember me?

8.

WOMAN: I don't think she remembers me.
MAN: What? Don't be silly. Her own mother?
WOMAN: It's alright. I'm just saying.
MAN: It's not alright, that's ridiculous.

WOMAN: Okay, maybe it's ridiculous.
MAN: I wish you hadn't told me that.
WOMAN: So do I, you're making a mountain out of a molehill.
MAN: It's nothing, that a child has forgotten her mother?
WOMAN: She'll come to remember us.
MAN: You think she's forgotten me too, then, do you?
WOMAN: She'll come to know us and love us all over again. We're starting again.
MAN: Five years down the drain, just like that, wiped away!
WOMAN: It's what it is.
MAN: No. I'm sure you're wrong. You're imagining things. I don't think it's possible.
WOMAN: I'm not upset about it, I'm just saying.
MAN: She'd have some vestigial memory, some subconscious—
WOMAN: Yeah. Yes.
MAN: So, you know, give her a chance. Give her the benefit of the doubt. For goodness sake!

9.

The MAN *watches the* WOMAN *commit to* LAURA.

10.

MAN: It's funny, being here, amongst all our old stuff, with her.
WOMAN: I know, it's as if the colour drained out of everything, and now it's back.
MAN: Same but different. Her.
WOMAN: Life and colour.
MAN: I feel I ought to smile when I come into the room.
WOMAN: Smile?
MAN: I never used to.
WOMAN: Why wouldn't you smile?
MAN: It's like trying to think of things to say to a person you've only just met.
WOMAN: You're crazy.
MAN: I am.
WOMAN: What's she doing?
MAN: Reading. That's what I mean, 'reading'?

WOMAN: Looking at pictures then.
MAN: Whatever, books.
WOMAN: Who wouldn't want their child to look at books?
MAN: It's funny though, to think of it. Laura with a book? Could you ever have imagined it?
WOMAN: She was four.
MAN: And half-monkey, we couldn't get her out of the mulberry tree.
WOMAN: What are you trying to say?
MAN: Nothing, I'm just remarking. It's good.
WOMAN: I'll finish doing this; why don't you play with her?
MAN: She doesn't want me to.
WOMAN: You got the shut-door treatment, did you?
MAN: She was more polite than that. I started talking to her …
WOMAN: Oh, well. Polite is good, and books are good.
MAN: You know I almost wish she'd have one of her horrible tantrums, the screaming and kicking and biting.
WOMAN: Are you serious?
MAN: I never thought I'd miss them. She was a handful, she was naughty, she told lies and stole choc-drops from the pantry and stamped on ants, but you know, that was her.
WOMAN: —
I'll help her get dressed.
MAN: Argh …
WOMAN: What, love?
MAN: You're annoyed. I shouldn't have said anything.
WOMAN: No I'm not.
MAN: I blame myself.
WOMAN: Why do you have to blame anyone?
MAN: You're right.
WOMAN: Be patient.
MAN: I blame myself for not being patient.
WOMAN: You've been through hell.
MAN: So have you.
WOMAN: The worst hell imaginable—
MAN: I know.
WOMAN: That morning; and then the insinuations, and the rumours—
MAN: Yep.

WOMAN: It's incredible that we survived. But we didn't split up, or throw ourselves under a train. Here we are, together.
MAN: Despite everything.
WOMAN: Yes.
MAN: But only because of you, because of your strength.
WOMAN: I had strength because I love you, you gave me the strength.
MAN: You held us together and I kept up the fight.
WOMAN: That's right.
MAN: I didn't rest, I never let her slip from the front page—
WOMAN: Yes.
—
What is it?
MAN: None of it made any difference. Any of that stuff, the TV appeals, there was never a single lead. She just showed up one day. Everything I did was meaningless.
WOMAN: It stopped you from going nuts.
MAN: I won't lie to myself.
WOMAN: Can you please be happy?
MAN: I'm trying.
—
—
I blame myself because of my expectations. I shouldn't have any expectations. Of her, or of me. The problem lies there. But all I wanted, when I wished so hard, prayed so hard, was our girl back.
WOMAN: And we have her.
MAN: Maybe a tantrum would be healthy.
WOMAN: You want it for your sake.
MAN: No, she needs to yell and cry and just get it out, whatever's in there. What *is* in there? The more she doesn't say, the worse I imagine it. Don't you? I mean the things I imagine, my God. Are we ever going to know?
WOMAN: If she needs to yell and cry, she will.
MAN: Now I wonder if we should have let them question her right then and there. At the time I couldn't think of anything worse, her having to relive it—
WOMAN: No, you were right.
MAN: They tried to convince me. I lost my temper, I went ballistic.
WOMAN: She needed to be protected, not dragged back through it.

MAN: But whoever took her has vanished into thin air, and our daughter doesn't speak.
WOMAN: You were reasonable: ten days away, we need that.
MAN: Maybe it was me, it was us, who didn't want to hear it. Maybe I did it for our sake.
WOMAN: Enough now, okay?
MAN: Okay.
WOMAN: She may not be speaking, but she can hear.
MAN: I'll stop. But it helps to say it.
WOMAN: It does.
MAN: —
All I wanted, when I wished so hard, was our girl back.
WOMAN: Yes, my love.
MAN: Now I know that can never happen.
WOMAN: What?
MAN: It can never happen because we've all changed: her, you, me.
WOMAN: What are you doing? Why can't you accept it? You'll pick away till there's nothing left!
MAN: Let me finish. They robbed us of that and it's gone forever.
WOMAN: What's gone forever?
MAN: Trust.
WOMAN: What?
MAN: I look at people in the street and I see liars and perverts. I don't believe in goodness anymore.
WOMAN: Then what do you make of the fact that she's here with us, in her room? If you want to pick away at everything, see what's under that: maybe you'll discover there's a God?
MAN: A God who let a child be stolen from her own bed.
WOMAN: And found again, nine months later.
MAN: Found, but—
WOMAN: Unharmed.
MAN: Was she unharmed?
WOMAN: Yes, the doctor said yes.
MAN: 'Wandering at large.'
WOMAN: Alive.
MAN: She doesn't talk.
WOMAN: Not yet.
MAN: And they robbed us of our daughter.

WOMAN: No.
MAN: She's not the same girl who disappeared that night, you can't deny it.
WOMAN: Stop it.
MAN: A piece of our lives, of her childhood, they stole that and we don't know this new person yet—please, listen, I'm trying to be honest—we don't know her and the little girl we once had,
WOMAN: Shut up.
MAN: That Laura's gone forever.
WOMAN: We're the lucky ones! What do you want, a phone call saying, 'We've found your daughter, safe and well', or 'Your daughter's dead'?
MAN: Yes.
WOMAN: Can you get that into your skull?
MAN: You're right. Thank you. Give me a good slap across the face.
WOMAN: Maybe you really don't know how to be happy.
MAN: I'd lose my mind if it weren't for you.
WOMAN: I think you would.
MAN: You see things clearly, everything's simple. Why do you stay with me?
WOMAN: The sex.
MAN: For her sake.
WOMAN: Everything is not about you.
MAN: I know that.
WOMAN: There's still a long way to go.
MAN: Remember what she used to do? When we argued?
WOMAN: Yes.
MAN: She'd get our two hands, remember?, from when she was tiny.
WOMAN: And join them.
MAN: Without a word. And it always worked.

11.

The MAN *mourns the absence.*

12.

MAN: What are you looking at?
WOMAN: Hmm.

MAN: What's she doing? ... Jesus Christ.
WOMAN: She's strong for such a small thing.
MAN: She can't do that! Why aren't you out there?
WOMAN: I wanted to see what she'd do with them.
MAN: How can you stand here and watch her destroying her things? I made that doll's cradle; she did those drawings for us!
WOMAN: I don't think she'll stop, even if you tell her to.
MAN: Then I'll make her.
WOMAN: Leave her!
  Please. I think we should let her.
MAN: Let her throw her toys off a cliff?
WOMAN: She's staying inside the fence, at least. She'll be doing stuff we don't understand, we have to let her.
MAN: Laura loved all those things!
WOMAN: Don't stop her, seriously.
MAN: Fine. But I can't stand here and watch.

13.

MAN: Hello.
  Can I sit in here with you?
  Here's Gerda. Remember Gerda? She hasn't been cuddled for a long time. Give her a little one, she missed you. I gave her some cuddles. But I'm sure she'd rather have one from you.
  Go on.
  Go on. Lovely Gerda. That's not how you hold her.
  We could go for a walk.
  We could go and look at your rock.
  It probably won't seem nearly so big to you now. Your island, remember you called it? We could wade out, don't tell Mummy, and play on it before the tide comes in.
  You look as if you've got no idea what I'm talking about! You can't have forgotten your island.
  I know, let's draw, draw Poppy for me. Because I want you to. You— You're right-handed, darling, don't you remember?
  Who's that, Poppy? With curly hair? He doesn't have a beard, I think you're making things up!
  Laura wait.

Knock knock. Who's there? I'm going to say 'six slithering snakes', do you know why?
—
—
—
—
Because I want to see if you've still got your lisp.
I know you're a big girl now but I'm hoping you do, I loved your funny little 's'. I'd be sad if it's gone forever.
What's that look?
Where are you going? Come here, come back.
Please, say 'six slithering snakes' for me, please just say it and I'll never ask for anything else. Please. Please.

14.

WOMAN: —how dare you, how dare you.
MAN: Stop, don't, shh, calm down, stop it, please.
WOMAN: I could rip your tongue out. Is that really what you think?
MAN: No! God no.
WOMAN: Then why say it?
MAN: Stupid.
WOMAN: Really stupid.
MAN: It popped into my head.
WOMAN: Then you should've kept it there. As if she doesn't have enough to deal with, without her own father heaping his shit onto her.
MAN: Oh. Please don't.
WOMAN: If you must have those disgusting thoughts—
MAN: I can't help my thoughts.
WOMAN: Then don't smear them all over me. Do you want me to look at her and think them? Why would you do that? I don't understand, you say you love me, why do you want to infect me?
MAN: I didn't say that's what I believed, I was merely posing a hypothetical.
WOMAN: Ugh!
MAN: We both said it, remember, we thought it the moment we saw her. You did too—you said it first. I was a bit shocked to be honest, but I didn't let it show, I agreed so you wouldn't feel bad.

WOMAN: No.
MAN: You said, 'My first thought was that's not Laura'.
WOMAN: Who else would it be?
MAN: No-one.
   But she picked up the pencil—
WOMAN: 'Evidence'?!
MAN: Don't overreact.
WOMAN: How could you test your own child?
MAN: I didn't set out to, it just, it occurred to me as a 'what if', 'wouldn't it be strange if?'
WOMAN: 'If this wasn't her.'
MAN: I know it's her, of course I do.
WOMAN: So why say it?
MAN: Listen, I'm happy to let it go.
WOMAN: Oh, it's me, is it? It's me trying to poison *you*.
MAN: No.
WOMAN: Why won't you let us just get on with things?
MAN: Come on.
WOMAN: Because when you say stuff like that, however ludicrous—
MAN: I simply put it out there, it's nothing, just a silly little thought, but I obviously hit a nerve—
WOMAN: I can't look at you. Never did I feel that way, trying to get you out of bed and off the grog, never once in the nine months after, but now—
MAN: Just remember.
WOMAN: What?
MAN: How it happened.
WOMAN: …
MAN: I never said it, I still won't.
WOMAN: You're saying it.
MAN: That's all: remember.
WOMAN: It was your job to check, it was always your job.
MAN: Why would I check a window that had never been opened since we moved in?
WOMAN: That's bullshit, whenever we burnt something—
MAN: You; I don't burn food.
WOMAN: I always opened it; are you really saying this?

MAN: I could have any time but I didn't, I never blamed you.
WOMAN: 'Blamed'.
MAN: And I still don't, I love you, it was a human mistake, I would never hold it against you, I'm just saying before you attack me—
WOMAN: You're low.
MAN: —attack me for words, just for a few words, consider the results of your action.
WOMAN: Do you think I haven't?
—
—
Do you?
MAN: No.
What's good about us, what I cherish, actually, is that we say what we think. We can tell each other—
WOMAN: Right.
MAN: Being able to unburden …
WOMAN: —
MAN: That's very rare.
WOMAN: —
MAN: I wish I could take that back.
WOMAN: It's out now.
MAN: We never used to argue.
WOMAN: Before this child pretending to be Laura showed up, do you mean?
MAN: I never had the urge to say that before.
WOMAN: Me burning the chicken, me leaving the window open? I was wretched, but I forgave myself. I'm sorry you can't.
MAN: We won't talk about it again.
WOMAN: Get over this and start taking care of your child.
MAN: Would you rather I pretended I was carefree?
WOMAN: Yes.
MAN: Well then, you've changed, because you always believed in the truth.
WOMAN: I don't care about the fucking truth or anything else, the only thing I believe in is her. I saw no point in going on when she vanished, but against all experience, all probability, all reason, she's come back. And I'll give up anything for her, including you if it comes to it.

MAN: My dearest one. Here. Shh. My darling. Forgive me. Please. You're right. Come here.
WOMAN: You can't do that, don't you see? You just can't.
MAN: I know.
WOMAN: It doesn't help.
MAN: You're trembling.
WOMAN: Promise, that whatever you're thinking …
MAN: I'm so sorry I said anything.
WOMAN: Yes. Me too.

15.

MAN: We need to have a little talk.
I want some answers please.
You are only five.
You are alone in the world.
You are very good.
You are traumatised.
You must have someone out of their mind with fear and worry, who'd give everything to be standing here as I am, with you.
You must look at us and long for them, we can't be any kind of substitute. Her room is foreign, her toys are objects, the rituals and magic words that were Laura's life are meaningless to you.
You are lost.
You are alone and good and traumatised and only five years old.
You are all these things, but you're not my daughter.
You are to be pitied, but you're not my daughter.
So where is my daughter?
Where in the name of Christ is my daughter?
And who are you?

16.

In the dark.

WOMAN: You're so far away, I can't reach you.
MAN: What?
WOMAN: You're all the way on the other side of the bed.

MAN: There.
WOMAN: That's better.
It never occurred to me that things would be, you know.
Like this. With us.
Everything else there was to imagine, every contingency, this just never—
When you said there was a stranger in the house, you were right. But you didn't go far enough: there are three. Three people I don't know. We're arguing about things that have never been an issue, I'm seeing a side of you— … And me: I was the little sister, young wife, new mother, always needing reassurance. When Laura went, I became rock-solid. I could hold it together because someone had to.
Then she came home and I thought, 'I can let go now. I can stop.' But there always has to be someone with no questions.
I wish … just for one moment, I could lean on you. That's all.
Sweetheart?
—
… Are you awake?

17.

MAN: That rose has a worm in it.

18.

> MAN: She brushes the girl's hair. They sit together, no need to speak. It binds them. It's an act of love, you can see it in my wife's face. Her heart's brimming over. A simple pleasure, and it's enough for her. What must that feel like?

The WOMAN *sings.*

> The silent communion. The giving and receiving. Her hair shines brighter beneath the brush, as if it's being burnished. The smell of her hair. A feather-pillow smell, human and sweet. To bury your nose in that hair, kiss the warm little head.
> And the girl, is she happy? Or does she just endure it?

WOMAN: Dad asked about next week.
MAN: What did you say?
WOMAN: That I think we need a bit more time.

MAN: Was he alright about it?
WOMAN: He was upset, actually.
MAN: Did you tell him why?
WOMAN: I tried.
MAN: What did you say?
WOMAN: Oh, you know, expectations. Surprises.
MAN: It's him we're doing it for.
WOMAN: Yes, but he doesn't see it that way.
MAN: Maybe we should throw him in the deep end, if that's what he wants.
WOMAN: I just couldn't bear—you know.
MAN: Everyone?
WOMAN: Yes, inevitable, sooner or later. You said it yourself.
MAN: I was playing devil's advocate.
WOMAN: Well, let's hold off while we can.
   Her hair smells the same.
MAN: You look tired.
WOMAN: Hmm.
MAN: Don't be worried, alright?
WOMAN: No.
MAN: I'm looking after you.
WOMAN: Why don't you have a turn?
MAN: You're better at it.
WOMAN: Here.
MAN: No.
WOMAN: Why not?
MAN: Do you want me to brush your hair?
WOMAN: Course she does.
MAN: She keeps turning toward the window.
   It's dark, there's nothing to see.
   What are you trying to see?
WOMAN: Are there stars tonight, Laura?
MAN: She's looking out, not up.
WOMAN: Here. Brush.
> MAN: I brush her hair and I can feel the enchantment working on me straight away. The golden threads. The way they cling to the brush, follow your hand, billow like waves. The warm little

> head, its perfect shape. I could sink into that pleasure, I want to stop thinking, nothing but the rhythm of the brushing, down and up, the gentle resistance, the sparks of electricity.

The WOMAN *sings.*

> Perhaps I could forget my daughter. Perhaps this child is enough. She's enough for my wife. She needs a home. I could learn to love her, couldn't I? We could let her take Laura's place. She may well have forgotten me, be living with some other couple, may be dead.
> This is how it feels to know nothing. To fear nothing.
> … Except her hair *doesn't* smell the same. Cloying perfume, like an old lady. As if someone else has been holding her. How can that be?

WOMAN: It's relaxing, isn't it?
MAN: Yes.
WOMAN: I can't keep my eyes open.

> LAURA *looks towards the window.*
>
> *The* MAN *goes to the window and looks out.*

What are you doing?
MAN: I saw something.
WOMAN: What?
MAN: At the window.
WOMAN: It's pitch black.
MAN: I thought—a kind of white blur.
WOMAN: A person? A face?
MAN: I—
WOMAN: What? What did you see?
MAN: No.
   No, just a reflection. That's all.
WOMAN: It's your hand with the brush, moving up and down!
MAN: Yes.
WOMAN: Please, sit with her. Brush her hair.
MAN: I—
WOMAN: For my sake. Please.
> MAN: I brush. I'm brushing out the perfume, sweeping away the evidence. Why do I feel weaker with every stroke?

I brush her hair and animals tumble out of it. Hairy dogs and muscular cats, a black crow, a wild swan and pigeons. A dog bites her hand; she takes the hairbrush and slaps the dog with it.
Look!
WOMAN: Beautiful, so shiny.
MAN: The animals escape by slithering through the floorboards.
WOMAN: Like a fairy princess.
MAN: All but the swan. It doesn't see the windowpane as it tries to get out, bangs against the ceiling. It beats its enormous wings above my head, twisting its neck in all directions, flapping frantically until the girl grabs it by the legs and thrusts it in my face.
I knew already this wasn't Laura, I thought it was just a terrible mistake. But if this is an innocent child, someone would be looking for her, she'd cry for her parents, she'd want to go home.
WOMAN: What are you thinking?
MAN: Trying to remember where I left my glasses.
WOMAN: Look at that glorious hair. My fairy-child.
MAN: That face. Not stupid, not naïve.
WOMAN: Laura darling, it's time for bed.
MAN: Her eyes, reading me.
WOMAN: Give Daddy a kiss goodnight.
MAN: She knows that I know. Her half-smile. She knows.

19.

WOMAN: He's going to check on her.
MAN: I pretend that I look in on her occasionally.
WOMAN: I wake up sometimes and he's checking on her.
MAN: In fact I never leave her side.
WOMAN: I look in, he's by her bedside.
I think it reassures him to gaze on her face, her little hands.
MAN: I'm waiting for her to give herself away.
WOMAN: The soft rise and fall.
MAN: She thinks she's too clever for me. The first night I must have dozed off. The second night I stayed awake, I saw her lips

moving. At one point her eyes flew open, but she didn't see me, she was looking over my shoulder, staring at someone.
Tonight she glitters in the gloom.
WOMAN: I hope it comforts him.
MAN: Tonight I'll catch her out; I don't need sleep.
Tonight she'll take me to Laura. I have their child, they have mine.
I won't move a muscle, I'll stand by the bed and watch until she …
Yes.
Gets up.
Bare feet.
Back door.
Black sky bristling with stars. I follow by their light.
She stops and listens. Obeying orders.
Barefoot through frosted grass, doesn't feel the cold of course.
And towards the gate.
Towards the edge of the cliff.
To receive orders, or to give them information or the human warmth she's sucked from us.
Her small feet blue in the moonlight, swollen and calloused.
Though not as small as Laura's feet.
She arrives at the place where grass becomes rock, where you can't hear for the boom of the sea and the spray wets your face.
She opens the gate and goes out.
She reaches the very edge. Will she float? Fly?
The very edge and stops.
Toes dug into the moss.
Listens.
Her lips move but I can't hear for the surf.
She's talking to them. Do they let Laura speak?
Now that I've discovered the truth, is she demanding more intelligence from my Laura?
Is she telling her how her mother dotes on a creature, has forgotten her own child?
And she laughs.
I hear that; deep and throaty, not my daughter's laugh.

Turns and walks right past me as if it's I who isn't real, I who's not human.
As she passes I look at her face
I look at her face
She's not a little girl.
No,
It's the face of a very old woman.
In the morning I won't show my wife the sand in the bed, the nightie green with moss, because she's not strong enough.
I'll get our daughter back and I'll never burden my wife with the truth.
Until then, I'll parade with a sick heart.

20.

LAURA *hands the* WOMAN *a book; her eyes on the* MAN.

WOMAN: [*reading*] 'Far away in the land to which the swallows fly when it is winter—'

    LAURA *turns the page.*

'… married a wicked queen, who gave them some sand in a teacup, and told them to pretend it was cake.'

    LAURA *turns the page.*

'… kissed the three toads and whispered to them, "Make her stupid, ugly and evil". As Eliza dipped her head under the water, one of the toads sat on her hair, a second on her forehead, and a third on her breast. But when she rose out of the water there were three red poppies floating on it.'

    LAURA *turns the page.*

[*To* LAURA] Do you want me to read this story?
—

[*Reading*] 'She rubbed Eliza's face with walnut juice, so that it was quite brown; then she tangled her beautiful hair and smeared it with disgusting ointment, till it was impossible to recognise her.
When the king saw her, he was much shocked, and declared she was not his daughter. No-one but the watchdog and the swallows knew her; and they were only poor animals, and could say nothing.'

LAURA *turns the page.*

'Oh! If she had only been able to confide in him and tell him of her grief. But dumb she must remain till her task was finished.'

MAN: What task is that?

WOMAN: We skipped that part.

MAN: Then you should go back and read it. Only wicked stepmothers skip pages. Only stupid fathers don't notice.

WOMAN: She wants you to read.

MAN: No.

WOMAN: Pardon?

MAN: My eyes hurt.

WOMAN: Because you're not sleeping. Why aren't you sleeping?

MAN: I can't.

WOMAN: That's not true. You're drinking coffee, you keep the light on.

MAN: No—

WOMAN: She's safe.

There was no-one outside. We can talk about it in front of Laura, she's more worldly than we are, no more codes and whispering. It won't happen again. So don't be afraid.

MAN: I'm not.

WOMAN: Oh.

MAN: No! No, I'm not worried about that.

WOMAN: Then, what?

MAN: I'd forgotten about that …

WOMAN: Your hands are shaking.

MAN: Stay up with me tonight. We can listen to music, or talk.

WOMAN: No, I'm tired.

MAN: But we haven't been together, just the two of us.

WOMAN: It's the three of us.

MAN: Please.

WOMAN: Look.

MAN: What is it?

WOMAN: She's offering you her hand, can't you see? Can't you see anything? What's the use of keeping your eyes open if you can't see, for God's sake?

MAN: Don't be angry.

WOMAN: Take her hand, sit with her, read.

MAN: In a minute, I'm going to make some tea.
WOMAN: Too late.
MAN: What?
WOMAN: She's gone to bed.
—
Well. Goodnight.
MAN: It's early.
WOMAN: I'll sleep with Laura.
MAN: No—
WOMAN: And you can keep your light on.

21.

The MAN *thinks of his lost* LAURA.
He reaches for her, and she's gone.

22.

The WOMAN *breastfeeds* LAURA.

MAN: Love …?
WOMAN: There's nothing wrong with it.
MAN: Oh, my God.
WOMAN: In some cultures they do it until children are eight, even ten.
MAN: Could you stop, please?
WOMAN: There's no milk, it's just for comfort.
MAN: It's not healthy.
WOMAN: Mine. My comfort. If it makes you sick, go somewhere else.
MAN: I'm asking you to stop.
WOMAN: Shh, my darling baby girl, it's alright. Shh …
MAN: I couldn't find you.
WOMAN: I need some space, you're following me like a shadow.
MAN: And this is why! Put her down.
WOMAN: No.
MAN: I have to talk to you.
WOMAN: Go on.
MAN: I can't with you doing that.
WOMAN: Then it can wait.

MAN: I'm serious.
WOMAN: If you can't say it in front of Laura, then don't bother.
MAN: Yes? You sure about that? Alright.
   Laura, this is going to give you nightmares—
WOMAN: Oh, for God's sake.
   Sit there, sweetie, wait for me.
   Well?
MAN: I want you to make me a promise.
WOMAN: A promise.
MAN: Yes.
WOMAN: What do you want me to promise?
MAN: That you'll tell me everything that happens.
WOMAN: —
MAN: Alright?
WOMAN: What do you mean?
MAN: Between you and her.
WOMAN: Like what?
MAN: Like *that*, what she was doing to you.
WOMAN: It was my idea.
MAN: That's what you think, is it?
WOMAN: —
   Here, you sit with her.
MAN: I'm dirty from the garden.
WOMAN: Sit her on your lap.
   —
   … Did you throw her off?
MAN: No.
WOMAN: Alright, well now that you've ruined that—
MAN: Love, don't be angry.
   Hey? Talk to me.
   What's the book about?
WOMAN: Green lacewings.
MAN: Sounds pretty.
WOMAN: They're parasites. They're destroying the herbs.

   LAURA *gazes out the window.*

MAN: Anything out there?
WOMAN: Do you expect her to answer you, with that tone?

MAN: I don't know what to expect.
WOMAN: Well, what are you going to do with yourself: just stand there?
MAN: Yep.
WOMAN: Peel the potatoes.
MAN: I could.
WOMAN: Do something.

A face at the window.

What's wrong?
MAN: Look.
WOMAN: What am I looking at?
MAN: You don't see?
WOMAN: No.
MAN: Come here—
WOMAN: Don't pull.
MAN: Look out there, quick.
WOMAN: Darling—
MAN: You've got to look!
WOMAN: You'll scare her.
MAN: No, I don't think so.
WOMAN: Go and do the potatoes, okay?
MAN: I'm not leaving you alone.
WOMAN: You saw a reflection.
MAN: It's light outside, there's no reflection.
WOMAN: You need to get some sleep.
MAN: I'm not going anywhere.
WOMAN: Fine. I'll start dinner, then.
MAN: Not yet, it's only four. Stay.
WOMAN: Well, I can't read with you interrupting all the time; you won't let me be with Laura.
MAN: Stay. Please.
Go on, read your book. I promise I'll be quiet.
And we'll play.
Alright? Can I join you?
That was a very clever trick you did.
Come to the window and show me what you were looking at.
Come on.
You were standing here, looking out.

Don't be modest.
And then how did you do it?

WOMAN: What are you doing?

MAN: Laura's showing me a trick.

WOMAN: Are you playing with her?

MAN: Yes, we're playing.
You stood here and looked out. How do you call them? What do you think to make them—

WOMAN: Laura sweetheart …
We might do some gardening. Grab your gumboots.

MAN: You're not going anywhere.

WOMAN: Can you see what you're doing?
Do you still care?

MAN: Yes! Yes!

WOMAN: How much longer?

MAN: I know.

WOMAN: Between her and you, I don't have much left.
Do something. Alright? You need to do something or we're going to fall apart.

MAN: What? What can I do?

WOMAN: That's up to you.

MAN: I don't know what to do.

LAURA *joins their two hands.*

… Laura?

WOMAN: She remembers.

MAN: Yes.

—

—

—

Or else—

He withdraws.

WOMAN: Oh, God. Oh, darling.

The WOMAN *leaves without his realising.*

MAN: Or they told her.
They told her what to do.

A SHADOW TWIN *embraces him from behind.*

Please. Dearest one. I know what I'm up against now. They're clever. But we love our daughter, and nothing's more powerful than love. I'll get her back again, I promise you. What matters is you don't drift away from me, they're trying to separate us, that's why you mustn't do that, milk or no milk.

Wait for me. I'll beat them. I only have to figure out how.

He discovers the usurpation.

LAURA *transforms.*

23.

Tantrum.

WOMAN: Oh stop, Laura, please stop!
MAN: Why is she having a tantrum?
WOMAN: I didn't peel the apple.
MAN: What?
WOMAN: She wanted some apple and I forgot to take off the skin.
MAN: I can't hear you.
WOMAN: Hold her.
MAN: I can't get near her.
WOMAN: Help me hold her.
MAN: Oh God, no more, make it stop, make it stop.

24.

A fury of intention.

The SHADOW TWINS *speak (singly).*

SHADOW TWIN: Let's have dinner in here tonight, it's much more soupy. Laura sweetheart, sit down next to Daddy.
MAN: What on earth is this?
SHADOW TWIN: We made it up. Breast milk, seawater, hair, and that's wet grass floating on top. Tea?
MAN: She pours the tea and sand comes out. What kind of tea is this?
SHADOW TWIN: Foxglove, of course.

MAN: She fills my teacup with sand, and waits for me to drink it. She doesn't think it strange because the creature has complete influence over her. She's bewitched her.
SHADOW TWIN: Too hot?
MAN: With those false little lovely eyes.
SHADOW TWIN: Too hot?
MAN: I can't drink this.
SHADOW TWIN: Laura, blow on Daddy's tea for him.
MAN: She takes my cup and gives me hers. I won't touch it of course, there's bound to be something revolting in it. Worms. Shit. Poison.
SHADOW TWIN: More already, sweetie? You've finished that? What a good girl!
MAN: And what's the main course?
SHADOW TWIN: More soup!
MAN: Out of an eggshell. Why are we drinking soup from eggshells?
SHADOW TWIN: You told me, cook the dinner in an eggshell. How else would I make it?
MAN: Great. Alright. Mm, delicious.
SHADOW TWIN: Want some more?
MAN: No thanks.
SHADOW TWIN: What about us?
MAN: Do you?
SHADOW TWIN: I might, if you twist my arm.
MAN: What?
SHADOW TWIN: Twist it. Go on, twist my arm.
MAN: No.
SHADOW TWIN: Here it is, go on, twist it.
MAN: No.
SHADOW TWIN: But Laura will have more.
MAN: Gosh. Must be hungry.
SHADOW TWIN: What a ferocious appetite! What a ravening little monster we have!
MAN: She's eating the shell.
SHADOW TWINS: [*together*] Well, she's very … well, she's very … well, she's very …
MAN: Very fastidious.

SHADOW TWINS: [*together*] Yessssssssssssssssssssss!
MAN: You don't mind if she eats yours?
SHADOW TWIN: And isn't she ugly? Look at that wrinkled skin, those bright black eyes! That enormous head. Just like an intelligent lump of wood.
MAN: I think—
SHADOW TWIN: We should beat her with a switch, a weeping birch is supposed to be best.
MAN: Oh?
SHADOW TWIN: Remember what a darling little baby she was? Legs as thin as chicken bones, and hands like a bird's talons, all covered with downy brown hair.
MAN: No, that's not what I remember.
SHADOW TWIN: And after just two weeks, a full set of teeth.
MAN: No. Really? No, my memory is that she was very, she was rather—
SHADOW TWINS: [*together*] She was rather … she was rather … she was rather …
MAN: Rather sweet, a rather adorable baby.
SHADOW TWIN: And me, I'm the rye-mother with long black tits and I'm coming to get you!
MAN: Oh …
SHADOW TWIN: I'm coming to get you!
MAN: Yes, but right now I'm eating.
More tea?
Oh … oh no …
The teapot didn't break!
The teapot fell and it didn't break!
The teapot fell and it didn't break!
 The room turns inside out.

25.

WOMAN: Your bag will have to go in the back seat.
MAN: Yes …
WOMAN: I've locked all the windows. Could you deadlock the door?
MAN: I didn't know we were going today. Did we talk about it?
WOMAN: I talked about it. I thought you were listening.

MAN: Oh, yes.
WOMAN: What are you looking for?
MAN: What?
WOMAN: What do you expect to see, looking around like that?
MAN: I didn't realise we were leaving ... no, but it's good.
WOMAN: I think it's time.
MAN: Yes, it gets a bit boring down here after a while, doesn't it?
WOMAN: Have one more look around the house to see you've got everything. I'll go and get Laura.
MAN: Um.
WOMAN: What's wrong?
MAN: Time for who, her or me?
WOMAN: I'm worried about you.
MAN: You've been on the phone, have you?
WOMAN: I don't think you're well.
MAN: I see.
WOMAN: You've been very strange.
MAN: I've had a lot on my mind.
WOMAN: Like what?

—
—

Like this not being Laura?
MAN: Yes.
WOMAN: It's worse than that though, isn't it?
MAN: Could it be worse?
WOMAN: You think she's some kind of ... impostor.
MAN: —
WOMAN: I've been married to you for ten years.
MAN: I'm not well? Is that what you think?
WOMAN: I won't judge you. Just admit it and then I can help you.
MAN: Why do you say she's an impostor?
WOMAN: That's it, isn't it? That's it.
MAN: —
WOMAN: I'm your wife, I love you. Say it so I can take you home instead, and look after you.
MAN: A breakdown.
WOMAN: I know it, I've watched you.

MAN: I—
WOMAN: Please let me.
MAN: If that's what you really think …
WOMAN: And everything will be okay.
MAN: But—
WOMAN: What, but what?
MAN: It's me, is that what you're saying?
WOMAN: Yes.
> How could we have assumed that everything would just snap back to normal? Nine months of living in hell, that changes you, we can't just shrug it off.
> It's not perfect, we're not how we were, but as long as you doubt her we'll never have her back.
> It's up to you.

MAN: —

> I think I did. I fell apart.

WOMAN: Yes.
MAN: I was lost, slippery edges, to look at her and not believe …
WOMAN: My poor darling.
MAN: And the shame, you know.
WOMAN: Yes.
MAN: That was unbearable.
WOMAN: It's alright.
MAN: And I couldn't tell you, I was so completely alone, I felt like I was going mad. It's been damnation. To distrust your own child. To look at your own child and find it hideous.
WOMAN: I wouldn't listen, it was me too.
> MAN: What if all this time it's been Laura, and she's innocent? Oh. God. The thought sucks all the breath out of me.
> —
> If she's innocent, then what am I?

WOMAN: That's all it took, you just had to say it. We'll leave, but we'll go straight home, I'll cancel the appointment.
> MAN: Then what am I?

WOMAN: Sit in the back with her. Sleep. When you wake up we'll be home.

MAN: Then what in Christ's name am I?

—

No. No. No.
No.
No.

WOMAN: I'll get Laura.

MAN: Wait.

WOMAN: —

MAN: Oh …

It's like a huge black bird's been crouching on my chest and it's lifted off and flown away.

WOMAN: You made yourself sick, you can make yourself well.

MAN: The relief … We're the lucky ones, I knew it but I couldn't understand it. Maybe it was all just too much to bear, like pouring boiling water into a frozen glass, and I cracked …

WOMAN: We can talk in the car, she'll be asleep.

MAN: I don't want her to sleep, I want to speak to her. I haven't spoken to her yet, not really spoken, this whole time I've been avoiding her.

WOMAN: We've got the rest of our lives. Come on, then.

MAN: Just before we go—

One thing.

WOMAN: What?

MAN: Let me take her for a walk.

WOMAN: Now?

MAN: Yes.

WOMAN: Not now, I want to get home before dark.

MAN: It's important to me.

WOMAN: Why?

MAN: Our ritual, remember? She and I would always go for a walk together before we left. I think it'd be a good thing to do.

WOMAN: Where, a walk where?

MAN: I don't know, down to the beach.

WOMAN: Well, let's all go. I could do with a quick walk.

MAN: Her and me.

WOMAN: I …

MAN: What?

WOMAN: Let's just go home.

MAN: What's the problem? I want to take my daughter for a walk. Why do I need your permission?
WOMAN: It's not that.
MAN: You've spent all this time together, you've gone for drives, you've cooked and played, but me—
WOMAN: I kept asking you.
MAN: I wasn't able to, now I am. Now I'm doing what you asked.
WOMAN: Uh.
MAN: Are you jealous?
WOMAN: Of course not.
MAN: You want her to yourself.
WOMAN: No.
MAN: There's never been a question of you taking her out, that we took for granted.
WOMAN: You're being silly.
MAN: Am I? Why don't you trust me with our daughter?
WOMAN: Trust?
MAN: What do you think I'll do?
WOMAN: It's not that, she's still so fragile, it's a responsibility—
MAN: You're calling me irresponsible.
WOMAN: Nonsense. You said you don't know how to talk to her—if I come—
MAN: I'll figure it out. Don't patronise me, love.
WOMAN: What am I supposed to do? Sit in the car?
MAN: Have a minute to yourself. You've been running around looking after everyone else.
WOMAN: How long …?
MAN: Dunno—not long.
WOMAN: If you walk along the road I can wave.
MAN: —
What do you want most of all? In the whole world?
WOMAN: My family. I want my family back.
MAN: Then you must have faith in me.
WOMAN: Yes.
MAN: You know that.
WOMAN: Alright.
MAN: Kiss me.

26.

MAN: Laura? My darling?
　Tell me what to do.
　Tell me what to do.
　　The MAN *rages against an invisible world.*

27.

WOMAN: Here she is.
　My beautiful girl, my dearest one.
　My darling.
　My love.
　My treasure.
　My angel.
　Do you want to go for a quick walk with Daddy?
MAN: Put the kettle on.
WOMAN: I'll see you very soon.
MAN: No time at all, I'll be back with our daughter before you know it.
WOMAN: I'll miss you.
MAN: And now,
　It's just us.
　You and me.
　Where shall we go?
　Take my hand.
LAURA: I thought you didn't like me.
　　MAN: That's not her voice.
LAURA: Did I do something wrong?
MAN: Hold my hand.
LAURA: You look sad.
MAN: I am a bit.
LAURA: Your hand's cold.
MAN: Come with me.
LAURA: Where are we going?
MAN: We haven't been to the rock yet.
LAURA: My island!
MAN: You know all about the rock then, do you?
　She loved her island.

LAURA: Who?
MAN: Laura.
LAURA: Yes?
MAN: So let's go for a paddle. Let's paddle out and have a play on it.
LAURA: You're not angry?
MAN: No.
   Take my hand. See?

THE END

GRIFFIN THEATRE COMPANY PRESENTS

GRIFFIN THEATRE COMPANY

SPLINTER

BY HILARY BELL

SBW STABLES THEATRE
6 SEPTEMBER –
12 OCTOBER 2019

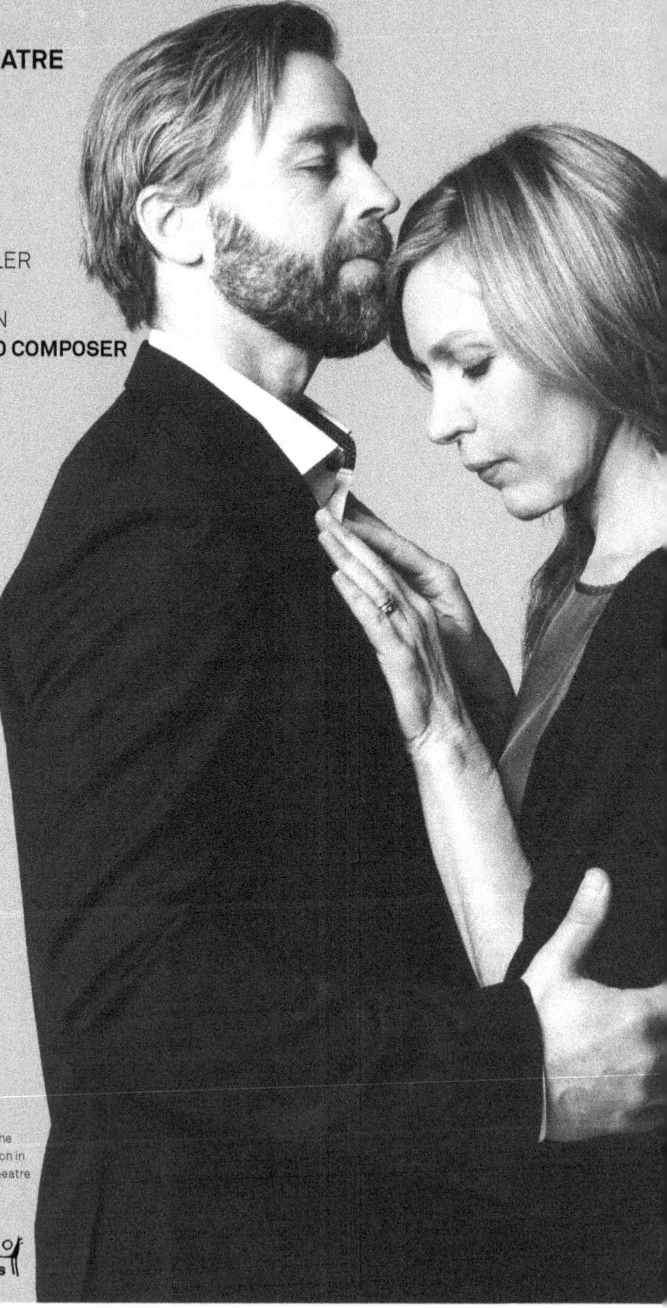

DIRECTOR
LEE LEWIS
DESIGNER
TOBHIYAH STONE FELLER
LIGHTING DESIGNER
BENJAMIN BROCKMAN
SOUND DESIGNER AND COMPOSER
ALYX DENNISON
VIDEO DESIGNER
MIC GRUCHY
STAGE MANAGER
REBECCA POULTER

WITH
LUCY BELL
SIMON GLEESON

Supported by
Griffin's Production Partner program

PRODUCTION PARTNER

Griffin acknowledges the generosity of the Seaborn, Broughton & Walford Foundation in allowing it the use of the SBW Stables Theatre rent free, less outgoings, since 1986.

Government partners

NSW Government
Australian Government
Australia Council for the Arts

PLAYWRIGHT'S NOTE

Splinter had its premiere in 2012 at Sydney Theatre Company, following a couple of intensive creative developments. It was a beautiful production co-directed by Sarah Goodes and puppeteer Alice Osborne, with guidance from dramaturge Polly Rowe. Originally commissioned as a work for children (!), it darkly bloomed into a kind of gothic thriller. I brought to the play two of my creative obsessions: fairy tales, and the Unreliable Narrator. My references spanned sources as diverse as Henry James' *The Turn of the Screw*, folk tales about changelings, the Grimm Brothers' *The Wild Swans*, Andersen's *The Snow Queen*, and a memoir written by Ed Smart about his daughter Elizabeth's disappearance. I was also intrigued by the idea of starting a play with what appears to be an ending: the restitution of a missing child. I had always wondered, when thinking about such cases, what life could be like following such a traumatic event. Can it ever return to normal? Do the effects ever vanish? How does a parent relate to a child who's been through the unimaginable?

At the core of the play's story is doubt, and its corrosive nature. Once the splinter of doubt enters the eye/heart/mind of the father—like the glass splinter in *The Snow Queen*—he's lost. The infection spreads. His wife is repulsed by his doubt, meaning he must hide it, which only feeds it. And once he can no longer resist it, and it takes hold, he must keep shifting the line in the sand in order to sustain his logic.

Splinter came to me pretty much whole. Unlike some other plays, where I've floundered, found myself becalmed, been filled with misgivings, I knew from the first instant what this play wanted to be. The final draft is not substantially different from my first outline. The writing work that followed was mostly a matter of putting flesh on the bones.

It's unusual for a contemporary Australian play to get a second life. I've never understood why this is so. Typically, we revive classics, we give new English and American plays a go, and we'll revisit a handful of older works from our own canon. But giving a new production to a recent play, even when it's been well received, rarely happens. A play takes a year of one's life to write, at the very least. Then, if it's lucky enough to get a production, that's four weeks of existence out in the world. And then it's over. It's a great investment of the writer's time and talents, of the originating producer's funds and energies, for a play to then vanish into thin air.

So, beyond the obvious pleasure at having a play programmed by Griffin, I feel a special joy and gratitude towards the Company for giving *Splinter* a second life. I'm sure all playwrights feel this way about their individual works, but with

Splinter, which consists of many open spaces and provocations, there is so much still to explore.

As times change, community attitudes shift and different echoes and highlights are revealed with each production. In the hands of new collaborators, a play becomes new again.

We acknowledge the importance of telling stories in order to understand ourselves as a culture—indeed, to create a culture. But perhaps it's worth thinking about the importance of *re*-telling stories. It's through constant retelling that children come to grips with how the world works (ask any parent who's closed a book only to be greeted with 'Again!'). It's how we measure the change that happens so subtly around us, we don't otherwise notice it. It also speaks to the very thing that distinguishes playwriting from other forms of literature: it is there to be endlessly reclaimed and reinterpreted for an audience.

Hilary Bell
Writer

DIRECTOR'S NOTE

Hilary Bell understands splinters. She writes at a level of detail and subtlety that is uncommon but often un-commented on. She has the power to take big ideas and slip them inside your head with a well-placed sigh, a strangely calibrated word, a uniquely tuned phrase, a killer half-sentence. She is able to detail the intimacy at the heart of all great love and violence. Her power is frightening. You wouldn't know it if you met her. You know it by sitting down late at night—possibly with a fortifying glass of something red close at hand—and reading her work. Humanity leaps off the page into voices that become moments that become stories that whisk you away to intense examinations of the human condition. Her nuance is addictive. I should know. I have been addicted to this play for years. It is a relief to put the words into the hands of great actors—if only to get the splinters out of my brain!

We don't do enough second productions of Australian plays—Hilary will probably talk about how devastating that can be for the long-term existence of Australian playwrights. I see it from the point of view of industry habits that are short-changing our audiences. Not every Australian play on our stages has to be new. There are some stories worth hearing again. Sometimes a new production will find a completely different way of realising the play that will connect with a whole new audience. It seems ridiculous to state such obvious thoughts. Yet we have got caught in the language of 'new' and 'first' and 'emerging' and 'world premiere.' We are missing out on creating new productions of plays we know are good, by writers who deserve to learn that the success of their play was not dependent on the success of that one prior production. New actors want the chance to play the roles, new designers want to reimagine the worlds, new directors always think they can do it better. Otherwise we would not have seen so many productions of Arthur Miller's plays!

In the last 20 years there have been so many fascinating Australian plays which have only had one production. It's time to look at our own bookshelf, maybe late at night, maybe with a glass at hand, and remember those plays and believe that if we would like to make them again, there may be an audience who would like to see them again. You tell me.

Lee Lewis

HILARY BELL
PLAYWRIGHT

As well as writing *Fortune* (1992) *Wolf Lullaby* (1996) and *The Falls* (2000), all for Griffin, Hilary's plays have been produced nationally by Belvoir, Black Swan State Theatre Company, Deckchair Theatre, La Boite, National Theatre of Parramatta, NORPA, Sydney Theatre Company, State Theatre Company SA, Darlinghurst Theatre Company and Vitalstatistix; in the US by Atlantic Theater and Steppenwolf; and in the UK by The National Theatre's Connections programme. These include *The Anatomy Lesson of Doctor Ruysch, Memmie Le Blanc, The Mysteries: Genesis* (with Lally Katz), *The Red Balloon, Splinter, Victim Sidekick Boyfriend Me, The White Divers of Broome,* and adaptations of Chekhov's *The Seagull,* Moliere's *The Hypochondriac,* and Shakespeare's *A Comedy of Errors*. She was Associate Writer on Paul Capsis's *Angela's Kitchen*, which premiered at Griffin in 2010. Hilary has written libretti for opera and lyrics for song cycles and musicals—most recently *The Red Tree* (comp. Greta Gertler Gold). Awards include the Philip Parsons Award, the Jill Blewitt Playwrights Award, Bug'n'Bub Playwright Award (US), the Aurealis Award, the Eric Kocher Playwright's Award (US), an Inscription Award, as well as a Helpmann and two AWGIES. Hilary is a graduate of the Juilliard Playwrights' Studio (US), NIDA, and AFTRS. She was the 2003-2004 Tennessee Williams Fellow in Creative Writing at the University of the South, Tennessee, and in 2013 was the Patrick White Playwriting Fellow at Sydney Theatre Company. She is also the creator, with artist Antonia Pesenti, of best-selling picture book *Alphabetical Sydney*.

LEE LEWIS
DIRECTOR

Lee is the Artistic Director of Griffin Theatre Company and one of Australia's leading directors. For Griffin she has directed: *The Bleeding Tree* (Best Director at the 2016 Helpmann Awards), *Prima Facie, The Almighty Sometimes, Kill Climate Deniers, Eight Gigabytes of Hardcore Pornography, The Homosexuals or 'Faggots', Rice, Masquerade* (co-directed with Sam Strong), *Gloria, Emerald City, A Rabbit for Kim Jong-il, The Serpent's Table* (co-directed with Darren Yap), *Replay, Silent Disco, Smurf In Wanderland, The Bull, The Moon and the Coronet of Stars, The Call, A Hoax, The Nightwatchman*. Other directing credits include: for Griffin and Bell Shakespeare: *The Literati, The Misanthrope*; for Bell Shakespeare: *The School for Wives, Twelfth Night*; for Belvoir: *That Face, This Heaven, Half and Half, A Number, 7 Blowjobs, Ladybird*; for Hayes Theatre Company: *Darlinghurst Nights*; for Melbourne Theatre Company: *Gloria, Hay Fever* and David Williamson's *Rupert*, which toured to Washington DC as part of the World Stages International Arts Festival and to Sydney's Theatre Royal in 2014; for Sydney Theatre Company: *Mary Stuart, Honour, Love-Lies-Bleeding, ZEBRA!*; and for Darwin Festival: *Highway of Lost Hearts*.

TOBHIYAH STONE FELLER
DESIGNER

Graduating from NIDA in 2005, Tobhiyah works as a designer across interior, architecture, installation and theatre projects. She's also a Lecturer in Design and Creative Practices subjects at NIDA. Set and costume design credits include: for Griffin: *Replay*; for Griffin Independent: *Lighten Up*; for ATYP: *Bustown, Desiree Din and the Red Forest, The Laramie Project, This Territory*; for B Sharp: *A View of Concrete*; for Bell Shakespeare Education: *Macbeth*; for Blacktown Arts Centre: *My Name is SUD*; for Ensemble: *Blue/Orange, Clybourne Park, e-baby, Good People, My Zinc Bed/Blood Bank* (for which her multi-purpose set design won the Installation Design Category at the 2016 Australian Interior Design Awards), *Sorting Out Rachel*; for Merrigong Theatre Company: *Camarilla*; for Musica Viva: *Da Vinci's Apprentice*; for NSW Public Schools Drama Company: *Bassett, The Elephant Man, Fugee*; for Performing Lines: *Variant*; for Riverside Theatres: *Parramatta Girls*; for Siren Theatre Co.: *Human Resources*; for Sydney Conservatorium of Music: *Daisy Bates at Ooldea, Orphée Aux Enfers*; and for Tamarama Rock Surfers: *Anna Robi and the House of Dogs*. In 2014, Tobhiyah was awarded Highly Commended Emerging Designer for Stage at the Australian Production Design Guild Awards. This year, *Flowstate*, a multi-arts outdoor performance venue for which she was a lead designer was awarded The Great Place Award by QLD Planning Institute of Australia. Tobhiyah is an active member of Australian Production Design Guild and is the Live Performance Coordinator for the MENTORAPDG program.

BENJAMIN BROCKMAN
LIGHTING DESIGNER

Ben is an award-winning lighting designer who works both nationally and internationally. Lighting design credits include: for Griffin: *Diving for Pearls, Replay*, 2016 and 2018 season launches; for Apocalypse Theatre Company: *Angels in America Parts I and II, Metamorphoses*; for Bontom: *Chamber Pot Opera* (Adelaide, Edinburgh and Sydney Fringe Festivals); for Darlinghurst Theatre Company: *Broken, Detroit, The Motherfucker with the Hat, Tinder Box, Torch Song Trilogy*; for Ensemble Theatre: *Baby Doll, The Big Dry, Neville's Island, The Plant, Tribes*; for Hayes Theatre Company: *Razorhurst*; for KXT bAKEHOUSE: *Dresden, Jatinga, The Laden Table, Straight, Visiting Hours*; for Legs on the Wall: *Cat's Cradle, The Raft* (Development); for Mad March Hare: *Belleville, Bengal Tiger at the Baghdad Zoo, Dark Vanilla Jungle, Eurydice, Shivered, You Got Older*; for National Theatre of Parramatta: *Girl in the Machine, The Girl/The Woman*; for Shaun Parker & Company: *King*; for Squabbalogic: *Good Omens The Musical, Grey Gardens The Musical, Herringbone, Mystery Musical, Man of La Mancha*; for Spark Youth Theatre: *Political Children*; and for Unhappen: *Animal/People, Awkward Conversations with Animals I Have Fucked, Cough, Mr. Kolpert*. Ben's portfolio and upcoming productions can be found at: www.benbrockman.com

ALYX DENNISON
SOUND DESIGNER AND COMPOSER

Alyx Dennison is a Sydney-based singer, composer and sound artist. She was one half of the critically acclaimed duo *kyü* alongside Freya Berkhout, and played festivals including The Great Escape (UK), Homebake, Meredith Musical Festival, Mona Foma Festival, and SXSW (US) before releasing their first studio album in 2010 through Popfrenzy/Inertia. In 2011, they were awarded the Qantas Spirit of Youth Award and disbanded on a high with the release of their second album in 2012. In 2015, Alyx released her solo debut album with Popfrenzy/Caroline, which she toured nationally, as well as supporting Deradoorian (Dirty Projectors), Juana Molina (Argentina) and LAMB (UK). As lead vocalist and instrumentalist, Alyx's performance credits include: for the Biennale of Sydney: *Composition for Mouths*; for Big hART: *SKATE*; for Liveworks: *Invisible, As Music*, *The Other Tempo*, *Rhetorical Chorus*; for Sydney Contemporary: *Bravi Brava Brave*; for Shaun Parker & Company: *Am I* (Tour). As Composer, Alyx's credits include: for All About Women Festival/Giant Dwarf: *Story Club Solo: Zoe Norton Lodge*; for Dance Massive: *CO_EX_EN*; for Dirty Feet/Dance Bites: *Double Beat*; for Next Wave Festival: *mi:wi*; and as Record Producer, credits include: for Bonniesongs: *Energetic Mind* (Smallpond UK); for Pheno: *Dragon Year* (Electric Ear Records); as well as current work on albums for Jessica O'Donoghue and Julia Johnson. Alyx is also a music educator, and has worked as a mentor for Campbelltown Arts Centre/Bree van Reyks's *Massive Band*; at Liverpool Girls' High School; and for *Wandering Books*, a music outreach program for refugee students in primary schools across Western Sydney. Alyx is currently developing her second solo release with the support of Campbelltown Arts Centre. She studied composition at VCA.

MIC GRUCHY
VIDEO DESIGNER

Mic works across stage, screen and video art and is a pioneer of video design for theatre. Mic's theatre credits include: for Griffin: *The Feather in the Web*, *King Tide*, *The Serpent's Table*, *Yasukichi Murakami–Through a Distant Lens*; for Brisbane Festival: *Freeze Frame*; for Merrigong Theatre Company: *Lost Boys*; for Monkey Baa: *Thai-riffic*; for Opera Australia: *Aida*, *A Streetcar Named Desire*, *The Girl of the Golden West*; for Perth Festival: *A Flowering Tree*, *My Bicycle Loves You*; for Performing Lines: *Wrong Skin;* and for Sydney Festival: *I Am Eora*, *My Bicycle Loves You*, *Puncture*. International credits include: for the Australian Chamber Orchestra at the Barbican in London: *The Reef*; for Jermyn St. Theatre, in London's West End: *Letter to Larry*; and for Satu Bulan/Performing Lines/Browns Mart Arts, touring across Indonesia and Australia: *Age of Bones*. Mic teaches Digital Media Design and Vision Technologies Production at NIDA and has lectured in media at Uni of NSW and Uni of Wollongong. Mic's video artworks have been included in collections such as MOMA in New York, as well as the Sydney Opera House, Sydney Olympic Park and the Biennale of Sydney. He was awarded an Australia Council Established Artist's Fellowship for Interdisciplinary Practice in 2012.

REBECCA POULTER
STAGE MANAGER

Rebecca is a graduate of NIDA (Production). Her credits include: as Stage Manager: for Arts Centre Melbourne/Critical Stages: *Songs for the Fallen*; for ATYP: *A Town Named Warboy*; for Darlinghurst Theatre Company: *The Mystery of Love and Sex*; for Ensemble Theatre: *Buyer and Cellar*, *Blue/Orange*, *Camp*, *Clybourne Park*, *Dream Home*, *Educating Rita*, *Luna Gale*, *The Good Doctor*, *Mothers and Sons*, *Relatively Speaking*, *Richard III*, *Two*, *Unqualified*; for Kay & McLean Productions/Sydney Opera House: *My First Time*; for Michael Sieders Presents/Adelaide Festival Centre/La Boite/Sydney Opera House: *The Very Hungry Caterpillar Show*; for Performing Lines: *Hello, Goodbye and Happy Birthday*; for Return Fire Productions/Comedy Theatre/QPAC/State Theatre Centre WA: *Senior Moments*; for Sydney Festival/Theatre of Image: *Brett and Wendy... A Love Story Bound by Art*; as well as various productions for Dead Puppet Society, The Hayloft Project, Milk Crate Theatre, MKA, Old 505, Q Theatre, Red Line Productions, Sport for Jove, Sydney Chamber Opera, Sydney Theatre Company, Tap Gallery and TRS; as Assistant Stage Manager: for Belvoir: *Strange Interlude*, *Thyestes*; for Malthouse Theatre: *Blood Wedding*; for Sydney Theatre Company: *Australia Day*, *Blood Wedding*, *The Comedy of Errors*, *Dance Better at Parties*, *True West*, *ZEBRA!*; for Sydney Dance Company: *CounterMove*, *Interplay* (International Tour); as Production Manager: for Adelaide Cabaret Festival/Chunky Move/KAGE: *Out of Earshot*; for CDP Theatre Producers: *The 91-Storey Treehouse*; for Ensemble Theatre: *Diplomacy* (Tour); for IPAC/Seymour Centre: *Cyrano De Bergerac*; for MTC Neon: *Dangerous Liaisons*; for Riverside Theatres/Sport for Jove/Seymour Centre: *A Midsummer Night's Dream*, *Romeo & Juliet*, *The Tempest*; as well as various productions for fortyfivedownstairs, Little Ones Theatre, and TheatreWorks; as Production Stage Manager: for Griffin: *Merciless Gods*, *Shining City*, *The Ugly One*; and as Technical Stage Manager: Melbourne International Comedy Festival.

LUCY BELL
WOMAN

Lucy has performed extensively on stage, including: for Griffin: *Dreams in White*, *Emerald City*, *The Falls*, *Speaking In Tongues*, *Wolf Lullaby*; for Bell Shakespeare: *The Duchess of Malfi*, *Pericles*, *Romeo and Juliet*, *Twelfth Night*; for Belvoir: *Blue Murder, Scenes from an Execution*, *Twelfth Night*; for Ensemble Theatre: *Marjorie Prime*; for Melbourne Theatre Company: *For Julia*; for Performing Lines: *Through the Wire*; and for Sydney Theatre Company: *As You Like It*, *The Cherry Orchard*, *Darling Oscar*. Film credits include *The Square* and *Ten Empty*, and most recently the award-winning short films *Second Best* and *Dots*. On television, Lucy has appeared in: for ABC: *Bastard Boys*, *Crownies*, *Dirt Game*, *Grass Roots*, *Magazine Wars*, *Rake*, *Wildside*; for the Comedy Channel: *30 Seconds*; for Nine Network: *Farscape*, *Here Come the Habibs*, *Love Child*, *Murder Call;* for Seven Network: *A Place to Call Home*, *All Saints*, *Catching Milat*, *City Homicide*, *Home & Away*, *My Husband My Killer*; and for Showcase: *Fighting Season*.

SIMON GLEESON
MAN

Simon's theatre credits include: for Cameron Macintosh Australia: *Les Misérables*–Australia; for Cameron Macintosh Ltd London: *Les Misérables*–London (West End); for Edinburgh Festival: *Certified Male*; for Gustave Stage Productions: *Love Never Dies*; for Melbourne Theatre Company: *An Ideal Husband*, *Hay Fever*; *Rupert*; for New London Theatre: *Imagine This* (West End); for The Production Company: *Chess*, *Curtains*, *Oklahoma!*; for Royal National Theatre (UK): *Southwark Fair*; for Shaftesbury Theatre: *The Far Pavilions* (West End); for Sydney Theatre Company: *Harbour*, *The Republic of Myopia*; for Victorian Opera: *A Little Night Music*; for Wexford Festival (Ireland): *The Silver Lake*, *Three Sides*; and for Sadler's Wells Theatre: *Shoes* (UK). Simon's television credits in Australia include: for ABC: *SeaChange*; for Seven Network: *Blue Heelers*, *City Homicide*, *Neighbours*. In the UK he played the regular role of Sid in *EastEnders* (BBC 1) and was a member of the principal cast of *Kombat Opera* (BBC 2) directed by Monty Python member Terry Jones. Simon also played the role of Ken in the feature film *My Life in Ruins*. Simon was awarded the 2015 Helpmann Award for Best Male Actor in a Musical for his performance as Jean Valjean in *Les Misérables*. He has received a further two Helpmann Award nominations and multiple Green Room Award and Sydney Theatre Award nominations for his work.

ABOUT GRIFFIN

"If you've ever sat in the theatre and thought, 'those actors are just too damn far away', then Griffin is for you."
– Concrete Playground

Located in the heart of Kings Cross— in the historic SBW Stables Theatre— Griffin has been dedicated to bringing the best Australian stories to the stage for the better part of four decades.

We're passionate about theatre that's written by Australians, about Australians, for Australians to enjoy. Iconic Aussie plays such as *The Boys*, *Holding the Man*, *The Heartbreak Kid* and *The Bleeding Tree* all had their world premieres at Griffin. And many of our nation's most celebrated artists started their professional careers with us— Cate Blanchett, David Wenham, Michael Gow and Louis Nowra to name a few.

Homegrown inspiration
By you, for you.

GRIFFIN THEATRE COMPANY
13 Craigend St
Kings Cross NSW 2011

02 9332 1052
info@griffintheatre.com.au
griffintheatre.com.au

SBW STABLES THEATRE
10 Nimrod St
Kings Cross NSW 2011

BOOKINGS
griffintheatre.com.au
02 9361 3817

GRIFFIN FAMILY

PATRON
Seaborn Broughton & Walford Foundation

Griffin acknowledges the generosity of the Seaborn, Broughton & Walford Foundation in allowing it the use of the SBW Stables Theatre rent free, less outgoings, since 1986.

BOARD
Bruce Meagher (Chair)
Simon Burke AO
Lyndell Droga
Tim Duggan
Lee Lewis
Mario Philippou
Julia Pincus
Lenore Robertson
Simone Whetton

ARTISTIC
Artistic Director & CEO
Lee Lewis
Artistic Associate
Phil Spencer

ADMINISTRATION
General Manager
Karen Rodgers
Associate Producer, Development
Frankie Greene
Associate Producer, Marketing
Estelle Conley
Associate Producer, Programming
Nicole La Bianca
Publicist
Jane Davis
Marketing & Development Coordinator
Lucy McNabb
Communications Coordinator
Ang Collins
Program & Administration Coordinator
Whitney Richards
Strategic Insights Consultant
Peter O'Connell

PRODUCTION
Production Manager
Ryan Garreffa
Production Coordinator
Dana Spence

FINANCE
Finance Consultant
Tracey Whitby
Finance Manager
Kylie Richards

CUSTOMER RELATIONS
Box Office Manager
Dominic Scarf
Bar Manager
Grace Nye-Butler
Front of House
Julian Larnach
Ell Katte
Ash Sakha

BRAND & GRAPHIC DESIG
Alphabet

COVER PHOTOGRAPHY
Brett Boardman

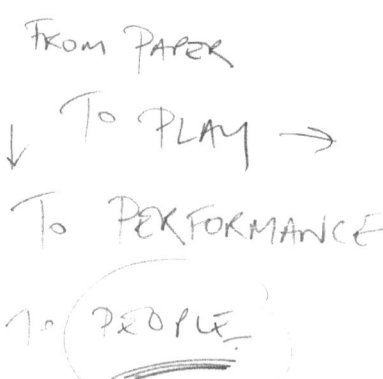

GRIFFIN DONORS

Income from Griffin activities covers less than 40% of our operating costs—leaving an ever increasing gap for us to fill through government funding, sponsorship and the generosity of our individual supporters. Your support helps us bridge the gap and keep ticket prices affordable and our work at its best. To make a donation and a difference, contact Griffin on **9332 1052** or donate online at **griffintheatre.com.au**

COMPANY PATRONS
Merilyn Sleigh & Raoul de Ferranti

PRODUCTION PATRON
Girgensohn Foundation

PROGRAM PATRONS
Griffin Ambassadors
Robertson Foundation

Griffin Studio
Gil Appleton
Darin Cooper Foundation
Ken & Lilian Horler
Malcolm Robertson Foundation
Geoff & Wendy Simpson
Danielle Smith
Walking up the Hill Foundation

Griffin Women's Initiative
Wendy Blacklock
Lyndell Droga
Sherry Gregory
Antonia Haralambis
Ann Johnson
Ro Knox
Ruth Ritchie
Simone Whetton
Lenore Robertson

SEASON PATRONS
A single exceptional production is chosen each season to be supported through our Production Partner program.

Production Partners 2019
Prima Facie
Robert Dick & Erin Shiel
Richard McHugh & Kate Morgan
Andrew Post & Sue Quill
Richard Weinstein & Richard Benedict

City of Gold
Ann & Brian O'Connell (in memoriam)
Andrew Cameron AM & Cathy Cameron
Bruce Meagher & Greg Waters
Julia Pincus & Ian Learmonth
Malcolm Robertson Foundation
David Marr & Sebastian Tesoriero
The Sky Foundation
Kim Williams AM & Catherine Dovey

Splinter
Stephen Fitzgerald

Production Partners 2020
Kindness
Pip Rath & Wayne Lonergan

SEASON DONORS
Front Row Donors +$10,000
Andrew Cameron AM & Cathy Cameron
Darin Cooper Foundation
Robert Dick & Erin Shiel
Girgensohn Foundation
Belinda Hazelton & Vicki Archer
Ingrid Kaiser
Malcolm Robertson Foundation
Anthony & Suzanne Maple-Brown
Richard McHugh & Kate Morgan
Rebel Penfold-Russell
Pip Rath & Wayne Lonergan

Main Stage Donor $5,000-$9,999
Anonymous (1)
Wendy Blacklock
Louise Christie
Lyndell & Daniel Droga
Danny Gilbert AM & Kathleen Gilbert
Helen & Abraham James & Family
Lee Lewis & Brett Boardman
David Marr & Sebastian Tesoriero
Sophie McCarthy & Antony Green
Bruce Meagher & Greg Waters
Peter & Dianne O'Connell
Sue Procter
Geoff & Wendy Simpson
Danielle Smith

Final Draft $2,000-$4,999
Gae Anderson
Baly Douglass Foundation
Lisa Barker & Don Russell
Helen Bauer & Helen Lynch AM
Ellen Borda
Marilyn & David Boyer
Bernard Coles
Alan Colletti
Bryony & Tim Cox
Lachlan Edwards
Gordon & Marie Fsden
Elizabeth Fullerton
Kathy Glass
Libby Higgin
Ro & John Knox
Kiong Lee & Richard Funston
Carina G. Martin
John McCallum & Jenny Nicholls
John Mitchell
Catriona Morgan-Hunn
David Nguyen
Anthony Paull
Julia Pincus
Chris Reed
Leslie Stern
Stuart Thomas
Tea Uglow
Richard Weinstein & Richard Benedict

GRIFFIN DONORS

Workshop Donor $1,000-$1,999
Anonymous (3)
Brian Abel
Antoinette Albert
Andrew Bell & Joanna Bird
Keith Bradley AM
Amanda Bishop
Michael & Charmaine Bradley
Dr Bernadette Brennan
Jane Bridge
Corinne & Bryan
Iolanda Capodanno
Peter Chapman
Sally Crawford
Cris Croker & David West
Nathan Croft & James White
Jane Curry
Timothy Davis
Carol Dettmann
Christine Dunstan
Ros & Paul Espie
Brian Everingham
Rowena Falzon
John & Libby Fairfax
Robyn Fortescue & Rosie Wagstaff
Jennifer Giles
Peter Gray & Helen Thwaites
Reg Graycar
Judge Joe Harman
James Hartwright & Kerrin D'Arcy
John Head
Danielle Hoareau
Mary Holt
Mark Hopkinson & Michelle Opie
Margaret Johnston
David & Adrienne Kitching
Jennifer Ledgar & Bob Lim
Richard & Elizabeth Longes
Elaine & Bill McLaughlin
Dr Steve McNamara
Kent & Sandra McPhee
Joy Minter
Kate Mulvany
Tommy Murphy
Ian Neuss
Ian Phipps
Martin Portus
Steve & Belinda Rankine
Steve Riethoff
Annabel Ritchie
Sylvia Rosenblum
Geoffrey Starr
Robyn Stone
Adam Suckling & Pip McGuinness
Augusta Supple
Peter Talbot
Sue Thomson
Daniel P. Tobin
Ariadne Vromen
Janet Wahlquist
Paul & Jennifer Winch
Simone Whetton
Elizabeth Wing
Kathy Zeleny

Reading Donor $500-$999
Anonymous (1)
Jes Andersen
Robyn Ayres
Melissa Ball
Nikki Barrett
Penny Beran
Cherry & Peter Best
Annie Bourke
Rebecca Bourne Jones
Simon Burke
Bill Calcraft
Gaby Carney
Michael Diamond
Max Dingle
Tim Duggan
Wendy Elder
Bob Ernst
Peter Graves
Tonkin Zulaikha Greer
Edwina Guinness
Con & Antonia Haralambis
Stephanie & Andrew Harrison
David Hoskins & Paul McKnight
Sylvia Hrovatin
Susan Hyde
Marian & Nabeel Ibrahim
Mira Joksovic
Anne Loveridge
Ian & Elizabeth MacDonald
Chris Marrable
Christopher McCabe
Wendy McCarthy AO
Patrick McIntyre
Nicole McKenna
Paula McLean
Neville Mitchell
Patricia Novikoff
Alex Oonagh Redmond
Carolyn Penfold
Judy Phillips
Malcolm Poole
Roslyn Renwick
Karen Rodgers & Bill Harris
Gemma Rygate
Jann Skinner
Rob & Rae Spence
Mary Stollery & Eric Dole
Catherine Sullivan & Alexandra Bowen
Pearl Tan & Priya Roy
Elizabeth Thompson
John Waters
Rosemary White

First Draft Donor $200-$499
Anonymous (12)
Nicole Abadee & Rob Macfarlan
Susan Ambler
Wendy Ashton
Penny Beran
Edwina Birch
Shay Bristowe
Peter Brown
Dean Bryant & Matthew Frank
Wendy Buswell
Ruth Campbell
David Caulfield
Charlie Chan & Angela Catterns
Peter Chapman
Sue Clark
Bryan Cutler
Owen Davies
Michele Dulcken
Dora Den Hengst
Dr June Donsworth
Elizabeth Evatt
Paul Fletcher
Lee French
Matt Garrett
Sarah & Braith Gilchrist
Deane Golding
Brenda Gottsche
Jennifer Hagan & Ron Blair
Elizabeth Hanley
Matthew Huxtable
Ann Johnson
Susan Kath
C John Keightley
Penelope Latey
Peta Leemen

GRIFFIN DONORS

Antoinette Le Marchant
Liz Locke
Maruschka Loupis
Dr Peter Louw
Carolyn Lowry
Anni MacDougall
Robert Marks
Guillermo Martin
Edward McGuiness
Duncan McKay
Ian McMillan
Sarah Miller
Sarah Mort
Mullinars Casting Consultants
Dian Neligan
Carolyn Newman
Gennie Nevinson & Vivian Manwaring
Peter Pezzutti
Meredith Phelps
Belinda Piggot & David Ojerholm
Marion Potts
Christopher Powell
Andrew Pringle
Virginia Pursell
Thelma Roach
Francis W. Robertson
Ann Rocca
Catherine Rothery
David & Dianne Russell
Kevin & Shirley Ryan
Julia Selby
Diana Simmonds
Michael Sirmai & Rebecca Finkelstein
Vanda & Martin Smith
Stephen Thompson
Jennifer White
Ruth Wilson
Eve Wynhausen
William Zappa
Aviva Ziegler

We would also like to thank Peter O'Connell for his expertise, guidance and time.
Current as of 15 July, 2019

SPONSORS

Government Supporters

Patron

2019 Season Sponsor

alphabet.

Production Partner

GIRGENSOHN
FOUNDATION

Griffin Studio & Griffin Award   Griffin Studio   Griffin Ambassadors & Artistic Associate Sponsor

Company Lawyers   Associate Sponsors

Company Sponsors

    Rosenfeld, Kant & Co.

MOPPITY   CURRENCY PRESS   Coopers   FOUR PILLARS   bourke street bakery

Access Partners

DESIGNKING COMPANY

Griffin Theatre Company is assisted by the Australian Government through the Australia Council, it's arts funding and advisory body; and the NSW Government through Create NSW.

www.ingramcontent.com/pod-product-compliance
Lightning Source LLC
Chambersburg PA
CBHW050026090426
42734CB00021B/3439